Europe

By Allan Fowler

Consultant
Nanci R. Vargus, Ed.D.
Primary Multiage Teacher
Decatur Township Schools, Indianapolis, Indiana

Children's Press®
A Division of Scholastic Inc.
New York Toronto London Auckland Sydney
Mexico City New Delhi Hong Kong
Danbury, Connecticut

Designer: Herman Adler Design
Photo Researcher: Caroline Anderson
The photo on the cover shows Germany's Rhine valley.

Library of Congress Cataloging-in-Publication Data

Fowler, Allan.
Europe / by Allan Fowler.
p. cm. — (Rookie read-about geography)
Includes index.
Summary: A simple introduction to the continent of Europe, including its geographical features.
ISBN 0-516-22236-8 (lib. bdg.) 0-516-25981-4 (pbk.)
1. Europe—Juvenile literature. 2. Europe—Geography—Juvenile literature. [1. Europe.] I. Title. II. Series.
D1051.F69 2001
940—dc21

00-057035

Printed in the United States of America.
3 4 5 6 7 8 9 10 R 10 09 08 07 06 05 04 03

The biggest pieces of land on Earth are called continents.

There are seven continents.

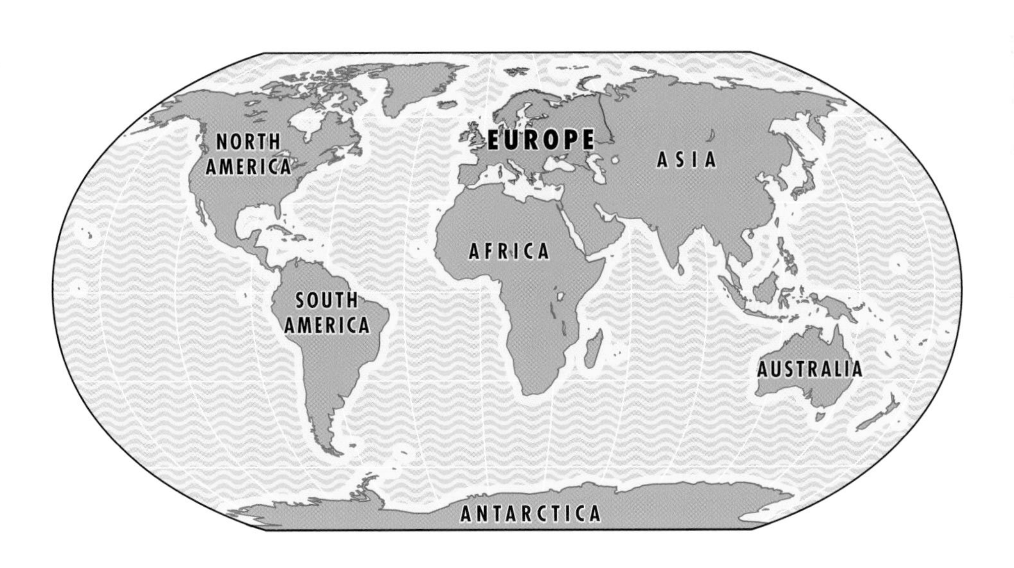

You can find Europe
(YOOR-up) on a globe.
It is much smaller than
Africa and Asia.

EGYPT
SUDAN
ETHIOPIA
ARABIAN
SEA
ZAIRE
ANGOLA
TANZANIA
KENYA

Great Britain is Europe's biggest island.

There are many countries in Europe. Some of them are islands (EYE-lands).

Islands are pieces of land surrounded by water on all sides.

Other countries are peninsulas (puh-NIN-suh-luhs).

A peninsula is a piece of land that sticks out into the ocean. It is surrounded by water on three sides.

Italy is a peninsula.

Parts of Europe are low and flat.

Netherlands

Some people built dams to stop the sea from flooding their low land.

High mountains cover other parts of the continent. Many people ski on these snowy mountains.

Switzerland

Some parts of Europe are very cold. Reindeer live there.

Saamiland

Cyprus

Other parts of Europe are very warm. People swim at the sunny beaches all year long.

There are long rivers
in Europe.

The Rhine River flows
through several countries.

In some European cities, the main streets are canals (kuh-NALS), or waterways. People travel around these cities in boats.

Amsterdam

Venice

There are many old buildings in Europe. The Colosseum (kol-i-SEE-uhm) was built almost two thousand years ago.

Many people travel to Europe's beautiful churches.

Others go to the Eiffel (EYE-fuhl) Tower.

Some people visit Europe's
grand palaces (PAL-is-es),
or castles.

The queen of England
lives in Buckingham Palace.

Europe also has many new things to see, such as the world's fastest train.

TGV

Europe is smaller than some continents. But it is filled with many places to visit!

Words You Know

Buckingham Palace

canal

Colosseum

continents

islands

Eiffel Tower

peninsula

Rhine River

Index

About the Author

Allan Fowler is a freelance writer with a background in advertising. Born in New York, he now lives in Chicago and enjoys traveling.

Photo Credits

Photographs ©: Corbis-Bettmann: 28 (Yann Arthus-Bertrand), 11 (David Cumming/Eye Ubiquitous), 16, 31 bottom right (Patrick Ward), 14 (Nik Wheeler); Nance S. Trueworthy: 5; Stone: 13 (James Balog), 4, 30 top left (Rex A. Butcher), 23, 31 top left (Hubert Camille), 10 (Tony Craddock), 22 (Simeone Huber), 27 (Chris Kapolka), 18 top (Bill Pogue), 20, 30 bottom (A. & L. Sinibaldi), 15 (Hugh Sitton), 18 bottom, 30 top right (Jamey Stillings), cover (Stephen Studd).

Maps (pages 3 and 31) by Bob Italiano.
Maps (pages 6, 9, and 31) by Joe Le Monnier.